IN INDIAN RAILWAYS, THE THIRD CLASS

MAHATMA GANDHI

Contents

THIRD CLASS IN INDIAN RAILWAYS

BY
M. K. GANDHI

GANDHI PUBLICATIONS LEAGUE
BHADARKALI-LAHORE

THIRD CLASS IN INDIAN RAILWAYS[1]

I have now been in India for over two years and a half after my return
from South Africa. Over one-quarter of that time, I have passed on the
Indian trains travel third class by choice. I have traveled up
north as far as Lahore, down south up to Tranquebar, and from Karachi to
Calcutta. Having resorted to third-class traveling, among other
reasons, to study the conditions under which this
class of passengers travels, I have naturally made as critical
observations as I could. I have fairly covered the majority of railway
systems during this period. Now and then I have entered into
correspondence with the management of the different railways about the
defects that have come under my notice. But I think that the time has
come when I should invite the press and the public to join in a crusade
against a grievance that has too long remained unredressed, though much
of it is capable of redress without great difficulty.

On the 12th instant, I booked at Bombay for Madras by the mail train and
paid Rs. 13-9. It was labeled to carry 22 passengers. These could only
have seating accommodation. There were no bunks in this carriage whereon
passengers could lie with any degree of safety or comfort. There were

two nights to be passed on this train before reaching Madras. If not more than 22 passengers found their way into my carriage before we reached Poona, it was because the bolder ones kept the others at bay. Except for two or three insistent passengers, all had to find their sleep being seated all the time. After reaching Raichur the pressure became unbearable. The rush of passengers could not stay. The fighters among us found the task almost beyond them. The guards or other railway servants came in only to push in more passengers.

A defiant Memon merchant protested against this packing of passengers like sardines. In vain did he say that this was his fifth night on the train. The guard insulted him and referred him to the management at the terminus. There were during this night as many as 35 passengers in the carriage during the greater part of it. Some lay on the floor amid dirt and some had to keep standing. A free fight was, at one time, avoided only by the intervention of some of the older passengers who did not want to add to the discomfort by an exhibition of temper.

On the way, passengers got tea tannin water with filthy sugar and a whitish looking liquid called milk which gave this water a muddy appearance. I can vouch for the appearance, but I cite the testimony of the passengers as to the taste.

Not during the whole of the journey was the compartment once swept or cleaned. The result was that every time you walked on the floor or rather cut your way through the passengers seated on the floor, you waded through the dirt.

The closet was also not cleaned during the journey and there was no water in the water tank.

Refreshments sold to the passengers were dirty-looking, handed by dirtier hands, coming out of filthy receptacles, and weighed on equally unattractive scales. These were previously sampled by millions of flies. I asked some of the passengers who went in for these dainties to give their opinion. Many of them used choice expressions as to the quality but were satisfied to state that they were helpless in the matter; they had to take things as they came.

On reaching the station I found that the ghari-wala would not take me unless I paid the fare he wanted. I mildly protested and told him I would pay him the authorized fare. I had to turn passive resister before I could be taken. I simply told him he would have to pull me out of the ghari or call the policeman.

The return journey was performed in no better manner. The carriage was
packed already and but for a friend's intervention, I could not have been able to secure even a seat. My admission was certainly beyond the authorized number. This compartment was constructed to carry 9 passengers but it had constantly 12 in it. At one place an important railway servant swore at a protestant, threatened to strike him, and locked the door over the passengers whom he had with difficulty squeezed in. To this compartment, there was a closet falsely so-called. It was designed as a European closet but could hardly be used as such. There was a pipe in it but no water, and I say without fear of challenge that it was pestilentially dirty.

The compartment itself was evil-looking. Dirt was lying thick upon the woodwork and I do not know that it had ever seen soap or water.

The compartment had an exceptional assortment of passengers. There were
three stalwart Punjabi Mahomedans, two refined Tamilians, and two Mahomedan merchants who joined us later. The merchants related the bribes they had to give to procure comfort. One of the Punjabis had already traveled three nights and as we

CHAPTER TWO

VERNACULARS AS MEDIA OF INSTRUCTION

VERNACULARS AS MEDIA OF INSTRUCTION

It is to be hoped that Dr. Mehta's labor of love will receive the serious attention of English-educated India. The following pages were written by him for the _Vedanta Kesari_ of Madras and are now printed in their present form for circulation throughout India. The question of vernaculars as media of instruction is of national importance; neglect of the vernaculars means national suicide. One hears many protagonists of the English language being continued as the medium of instruction pointing to the fact that English-educated Indians are the sole custodians of public and patriotic work. It would be monstrous if it were not so. The only education given in this country is through the English language. The fact, however, is that the results are not all proportionate to the time we give to our education. We have not reacted to the masses. But I must not anticipate Dr. Mehta. He is in earnest. He writes feelingly. He has examined the pros and cons and collected a mass of evidence in support of his arguments. The latest pronouncement on the subject is that of the Viceroy. Whilst His Excellency is unable to offer a solution, he is keenly alive to the necessity of imparting instruction in our schools through the vernaculars. The Jews of Middle and Eastern Europe, who are scattered in all parts of the world, finding it necessary to have a common tongue for mutual intercourse, have raised Yiddish to the status of a language, and have succeeded in translating into Yiddish the best books to be found in the world's literature. Even they could not satisfy the soul's yearning through the many foreign tongues of which they are masters; nor did the learned few among them wish to tax the masses of the Jewish population with having to learn a foreign language before they could realize their dignity. So they have enriched what was at one time looked upon as a mere jargon--but what the Jewish children learned from their mothers--by taking special pains to translate into it the best thought of the world. This is a truly marvelous work. It has been done during the present generation, and Webster's Dictionary defines it as a polyglot jargon used for inter-communication by Jews from different nations.

But a Jew of Middle and Eastern Europe would feel insulted if his mother tongue were now so described. If these Jewish scholars have succeeded, within a generation, in giving their masses a language of which they may feel proud, surely it should be an easy task for us to supply the needs of our vernaculars which are cultured languages. South Africa teaches us the same lesson. There was a duel there between the Taal, a corrupt form of Dutch, and English. The Boer mothers and the Boer fathers were determined that they would not let their children, with whom they in their infancy talked in the Taal, be weighed down with having to receive instruction through English. The case for English here was a strong one. It had able pleaders for it. But English had to yield before Boer's patriotism. It may be observed that they rejected even the High Dutch. The schoolmasters, therefore, who are accustomed to speaking the published Dutch of Europe, are compelled to teach the easier Taal. And the literature of an excellent character is at the present moment growing up in South Africa in the Taal, which was only a few years ago, the common medium of speech between simple but brave rustics. If we have lost faith in our vernaculars, it is a sign of want of faith in ourselves; it is the surest sign of decay. And no scheme of self-government, however benevolently or generously it may be bestowed upon us, will ever make us a self-governing nation, if we have no respect for the languages our mothers speak.

FOOTNOTE:

[2] Introduction to Dr. Mehta's "Self-Government Series".

CHAPTER THREE

SWADESHI

SWADESHI

It was not without great diffidence that I undertook to speak to you at
all. And I was hard put to it in the selection of my subject. I have
chosen a very delicate and difficult subject. It is delicate because of
the peculiar views I hold upon Swadeshi, and it is difficult because I
have not that command of language which is necessary for giving adequate
expression to my thoughts. I know that I may rely upon your indulgence
for the many shortcomings you will no doubt find in my address, the more
so when I tell you that there is nothing in what I am about to say that
I am not either already practicing or am not preparing to practice to
the best of my ability. It encourages me to observe that last month you
devoted a week to prayer in the place of an address. I have earnestly
prayed that what I am about to say may bear fruit and I know that you
will bless my word with a similar prayer.

After much thinking, I have arrived at a definition of Swadeshi that,
perhaps, best illustrates my meaning. Swadeshi is that spirit in us
that restricts us to the use and service of our immediate surroundings
to the exclusion of the more remote. Thus, as for religion, to
satisfy the requirements of the definition, I must restrict myself to my
ancestral religion. That is the use of my immediate religious
surrounding. If I find it defective, I should serve it by purging it of
its defects. In the domain of politics, I should make use of the
indigenous institutions and serve them by curing them of their proved
defects. In that economics, I should use only things that are produced
by my immediate neighbors and serve those industries by making them
efficient and complete where they might be found wanting. It is
suggested that such Swadeshi if reduced to practice, will lead to the

millennium. And, as we do not abandon our pursuit after the millennium, because we do not expect quite to reach it within our times, so may we not abandon Swadeshi even though it may not be fully attained for generations to come.

Let us briefly examine the three branches of Swadeshi as sketched above. Hinduism has become a conservative religion and, therefore, a mighty force because of the Swadeshi spirit underlying it. It is the most tolerant because it is non-proselytizing, and it is as capable of expansion today as it is in the past. It has succeeded not in driving out, as I think it has been erroneously held, but in absorbing Buddhism. Because of the Swadeshi spirit, a Hindu refuses to change his religion, not necessarily because he considers it to be the best, but because he knows that he can complement it by introducing reforms. And what I have said about Hinduism is, I suppose, true of the other great faiths of the world, only it is held that it is especially so in the case of Hinduism. But here comes the point I am laboring to reach. If there is any substance in what I have said, will not the great missionary bodies of India, to whom she owes a deep debt of gratitude for what they have done and are doing, do still better and serve the spirit of Christianity better by dropping the goal of proselytizing while continuing their philanthropic work? I hope you will not consider this to be an impertinence on my part. I suggest all sincerity and with due humility. Moreover, I have some claims for your attention. I have endeavored to study the Bible. I consider it as part of my scriptures. The spirit of the Sermon on the Mount competes almost on equal terms with the Bhagavad Gita for the domination of my heart. I yield to no Christian in the strength of devotion with which I sing "Lead kindly light" and several other inspired hymns of a similar nature. I have come under the influence of noted Christian missionaries belonging to different denominations. And enjoy to this day the privilege of friendship with some of them. You will perhaps, therefore, allow that I have offered the above suggestion not as a biased Hindu, but as a humble and impartial student of religion with a great leaning toward Christianity. May it is not that "Go ye unto all the world" the message has been somewhat narrowly interpreted and the spirit of it missed? It will not be denied, I speak from experience, that many of the conversions are only so-called. In some cases, the appeal has gone not to the heart but the stomach. And in every case, a conversion leaves a sore behind it which, I venture to think, is avoidable. Quoting again from experience, a new birth, a change of heart, is perfectly possible in every one of the great faiths. I know I am now treading upon thin ice. But I do not apologize in closing this part of my subject, for saying that the frightful outrage that is just going on in Europe, perhaps shows that the message of Jesus of Nazareth, the Son of Peace, had been little understood in Europe, and that light upon it may have to be thrown from the East.

I have sought your help in religious matters, which it is your

CHAPTER FOUR

AHINSA

AHINSA

There seems to be no historical warrant for the belief that an
exaggerated practice of Ahimsa synchronizes with our becoming bereft of
manly virtues. During the past 1,500 years, we have, as a nation, given
ample proof of physical courage, but we have been torn by internal
dissensions and have been dominated by the love of self instead of love of
country. We have, that is to say, been swayed by the spirit of
irreligion rather than of religion.

I do not know how far the charge of unmanliness can be made good
against
the Jains. I hold no brief for them. By birth, I am a Vaishnavite and
was taught Ahimsa in my childhood. I have derived much religious benefit
from Jain religious works as I have from scriptures of the other great
faiths of the world. I owe much to the living company of the deceased
philosopher, Rajachand Kavi, who was a Jain by birth. Thus, though my
views on Ahimsa are a result of my study of most of the faiths of the
world, they are now no longer dependent upon the authority of these
works. They are a part of my life, and, if I suddenly discovered that
the religious books read by me bore a different interpretation from the
one I had learned to give them, I should still hold to the view of Ahimsa
as I am about to set forth here.

Our Shastras seem to teach that a man who practices Ahimsa in its
fulness has the world at his feet; he so affects his surroundings that
even the snakes and other venomous reptiles do him no harm. This is said
to have been the experience of St. Francis of Assisi.

In its negative form, it means not injuring any living being whether by
body or mind. It may not, therefore, hurt the person of any wrong-doer,

or bear any ill-will to him and so cause him mental suffering. This statement does not cover suffering caused to the wrong-doer by natural acts of mine which do not proceed from ill-will. It, therefore, does not prevent me from withdrawing from his presence a child whom he, we shall imagine, is about to strike. Indeed, the proper practice of Ahimsa _requires_ me to withdraw the intended victim from the wrong-doer, if I am, in any way whatsoever, the guardian of such a child. It was, therefore, most proper for the passive resisters of South Africa to have resisted the evil that the Union Government sought to do to them. They bore no ill-will to it. They showed this by helping the Government whenever it needed their help. _Their resistance consisted of disobedience of the orders of the Government, even to the extent of suffering death at their hands._ Ahimsa requires deliberate self-suffering, not a deliberate injury of the supposed wrong-doer.

In its positive form, Ahimsa means the largest love, the greatest charity. If I am a follower of Ahimsa, I _must love_, my enemy. I must apply the same rules to the wrong-doer who is my enemy or a stranger to me, as I would to my wrong-doing father or son. This active Ahimsa necessarily includes truth and fearlessness. As man cannot deceive the loved one, he does not fear or frighten him or her. The gift of life is the greatest of all gifts; a man who gives it, in reality, disarms all hostility. He has paved the way for an honorable understanding. And none who is himself subject to fear can bestow that gift. He must, therefore, be fearless. A man cannot then practice Ahimsa and be a coward at the same time. The practice of Ahimsa calls forth the greatest courage. It is the most soldierly of a soldier's virtues. General Gordon has been represented in a famous statue as bearing only a stick. This takes us far on the road to Ahimsa. But a soldier, who needs the protection of even a stick, is to that extent so much the less a soldier. He is the true soldier who knows how to die and stand his ground amid a hail of bullets. Such a one was Ambarisha, who stood his ground without lifting a finger through Duryasa and did his worst. The Moors who were being pounded by the French gunners and who rushed to
the guns' mouths with 'Allah' on their lips, showed much the same type of courage. Only theirs was the courage of desperation. Ambarisha's was due to love. Yet the Moorish valor, readiness to die, conquered the gunners. They frantically waved their hats, ceased firing, and greeted

their erstwhile enemies as comrades. And so the South African passive resisters in their thousands were ready to die rather than sell their honor for a little personal ease. This was Ahimsa in its active form. It _never_ barters away honor. A helpless girl in the hands of a follower of Ahimsa finds better and surer protection than in the hands of one who is prepared to defend her only to the point to which his weapons would carry him. The tyrant, in the first instance, will have to walk to his victim over the dead body of her defender; in the second, he has but to overpower the defender; for it is assumed that the cannon of propriety in the second instance will be satisfied when the defender has fought to the extent of his physical valor. In the first instance, as the defender has matched his very soul against the mere body of the tyrant, the odds are that the soul in the latter will be awakened, and the girl would stand an infinitely greater chance of her honor being protected than in any other conceivable circumstance, barring of course, that of her courage.

If we are unmanly today, we are so, not because we do not know how to strike, but because we fear dying. He is no follower of Mahavira, the apostle of Jainism, or Buddha or of the Vedas, who is afraid to die, takes flight before any danger, real or imaginary, all the while wishing that somebody else would remove the danger by destroying the the person causing it. He is no follower of Ahimsa who does not care about a straw if he kills a man by inches by deceiving him in trade, who would protect by force of arms a few cows and make away with the butcher or who, to do a supposed good to his country, does not mind killing off a few officials. All these are actuated by hatred, cowardice, and fear. Here the love of the cow or the country is a vague thing intended to satisfy one's vanity or soothe a stinging conscience.

Ahimsa truly understood is in my humble opinion a panacea for all evils mundane and extra-mundane. We can never overdo it. Just at present, we are not doing it at all. Ahimsa does not displace the practice of other virtues but renders their practice imperatively necessary before it can be practiced even in its rudiments. Mahavira and Buddha were soldiers, and so was Tolstoy. Only they saw deeper and truer into their profession and found the secret of a true, happy, honorable, and godly life. Let us be joint sharers with these teachers, and this land of ours will once more be the abode of gods.

FOOTNOTE:

[4] The _Modern Review_, October 1916.

CHAPTER FIVE

THE MORAL BASIS OF CO-OPERATION

THE MORAL BASIS OF CO-OPERATION

The only claim I have on your indulgence is that some months ago I attended with Mr. Ewbank a meeting of mill-hands to whom he wanted to explain the principles of co-operation. The chawl in which they were living was as filthy as it well could be. Recent rains had made matters worse. And I must frankly confess that, had it not been for Mr. Ewbank's great zeal for the cause he has made his own, I should have shirked the task. But there we were, seated on a fairly worn-out _charpai_, surrounded by men, women, and children. Mr. Ewbank opened fire on a man
who had put himself forward and who wore not a particularly innocent countenance. After he had engaged him and the other people about him in Gujrati conversation, he wanted me to speak to the people. Owing to the suspicious looks of the man who was first spoken to, I naturally pressed home the moralities of co-operation. I fancy that Mr. Ewbank rather liked how I handled the subject. Hence, I believe, his
kind invitation to me to tax your patience for a few moments upon consideration of co-operation from a moral standpoint.

My knowledge of the technicality of co-operation is next to nothing. My brother, Devadhar, has made the subject his own. Whatever he does, naturally attracts me and predisposes me to think that there must be something good in it and the handling of it must be fairly difficult. Mr. Ewbank very kindly placed at my disposal some literature too on the subject. And I have had a unique opportunity of watching the effect of some co-operative effort in Champaran. I have gone through Mr. Ewbank's ten main points which are like the Commandments, and I have gone through the twelve points of Mr. Collins of Behar, which remind me of the law of the Twelve Tables. There are so-called agricultural banks in Champaran. They were to me disappointing efforts if they were meant to be demonstrations of the success of co-operation. On the other hand, there is quiet work in the same direction being done by Mr. Hodge, a missionary whose efforts are leaving their impress on those who come in contact with him. Mr. Hodge is a co-operative enthusiast and probably considers that the result which he sees flowing from his efforts are due to the working of co-operation. I, who was able to watch the efforts, had no hesitation in inferring that the personal equation counted for success in the one and failure in the other instance.

I am an enthusiast myself, but twenty-five years of experimenting and experience has made me a cautious and discriminating enthusiast. Workers in a cause necessarily, though quite unconsciously, exaggerate its merits and often succeed in turning its very defects into advantages. Despite my caution, I consider the little institution I am conducting in Ahmedabad as the finest thing in the world. It alone gives me sufficient inspiration. Critics tell me that it represents a soulless soul-force and that its severe discipline has made it merely mechanical. I suppose both--the critics and I--are wrong. It is, at best, a humble attempt to place at the disposal of the nation a home where men and women may have scope for free and unfettered development of character, in keeping with the national genius, and, if its controllers do not take care, the discipline that is the foundation of character may frustrate the very end in view. I would venture, therefore, to warn enthusiasts in co-operation against entertaining false hopes.

With Sir Daniel Hamilton it has become a religion. On the 13th of January last, he addressed the students of the Scottish Churches College and, to point out a moral, he instanced Scotland's poverty of two hundred years ago and showed how that great country was raised from a condition of poverty to plenty. "There were two powers, which raised her--the Scottish Church and the Scottish banks. The Church manufactured the men and the banks manufactured the money to give the men a start in life... The Church disciplined the nation in the fear of God which is the beginning of wisdom and in the parish schools of the Church, the children learned that the chief end of man's life was to glorify God and to enjoy Him forever. Men were trained to believe in God and themselves, and on the trustworthy character so created the Scottish banking system was built." Sir Daniel then shows that it was possible to build up the marvelous Scottish banking system only on the character so built. So far there can only be a perfect agreement with Sir Daniel, for that 'without character there is no co-operation' is a sound maxim. But he would have us go much further. He thus waxes eloquent on co-operation: "Whatever may be your daydreams of India's future, never forget this that it is to weld India into one, and so enable her to take her rightful place in the world, that the British Government is here; and the welding hammer in the hand of the Government is the co-operative movement." In his opinion

CHAPTER SIX

NATIONAL DRESS

NATIONAL DRESS

I have hitherto successfully resisted the temptation of either answering your or Mr. Irwin's criticism of the humble work I am doing in Champaran. Nor am I going to succumb now except about a matter which Mr. Irwin has thought fit to dwell upon and about which he has not even taken the trouble of being correctly informed. I refer to his remarks on my manner of dressing.

My "familiarity with the minor amenities of Western civilization" has taught me to respect my national costume, and it may interest Mr. Irwin to know that the dress I wear in Champaran is the dress I have always worn in India except that for a very short period in India I fell an easy prey in common with the rest of my countrymen to the wearing of semi-European dress in the courts and elsewhere outside Kathiawar. I appeared before the Kathiawar courts now 21 years ago in precisely the the dress I wear in Champaran.

One change I have made is that having taken to the occupation of weaving and agriculture and having taken the vow of Swadeshi, my clothing is now entirely hand-woven and hand-sewn and made by me or my fellow workers. Mr. Irwin's letter suggests that I appear before the ryots in a dress I have temporarily and specially adopted in Champaran to produce an effect. The fact is that I wear the national dress because it is the most natural and the most becoming for an Indian. I believe that our copying of the European dress is a sign of our degradation, humiliation, and our weakness and that we are committing a national sin in discarding a dress that is best suited to the Indian climate and which, for its simplicity, art, and cheapness, is not to be beaten on the face of the earth and which answers hygienic requirements. Had it not been for false pride and equally false notions of prestige, Englishmen here would long ago have adopted the Indian costume. I may mention incidentally that I do not go about Champaran bareheaded. I do avoid shoes for sacred reasons. But I find too that it is more natural and healthier to avoid them whenever possible.

I am sorry to inform Mr. Irwin and your readers that my esteemed friend Babu Brijakishore Prasad, the "ex-Hon. Member of Council," remains unregenerate and retains the provincial cap and never walks barefoot and "kicks up" a terrible noise even in the house we are living in by wearing wooden sandals. He has still not the courage, despite most admirable contact with me, to discard his semi-anglicized dress and whenever he goes to see officials he puts his legs into the bifurcated garment and on his admission tortures himself by cramping his feet in inelastic shoes. I cannot induce him to believe that his clients won't desert him and the courts won't punish him if he wore his more becoming and less expensive dhoti. I invite you and Mr. Irwin not to believe the "stories" that the latter hears about me and my friends, but to join me in the crusade against educated Indians abandoning their manners, habits, and customs which are not proved to be bad or harmful. Finally, I venture to warn you and Mr. Irwin that you and he will ill-serve the cause both of you consider is in danger because of my presence in Champaran if you continue, as you have done, to base your strictures on unproven facts. I ask you to accept my assurance that I should deem myself unworthy of the friendship and confidence of hundreds of my English friends and associates--not all of them fellow cranks--if in similar circumstances, I acted toward them differently from my own countrymen.

FOOTNOTE:

[6] Reply to Mr. Irwin's criticism of his dress in the _Pioneer_.

Printed by K. R. Sondhi at the Allied Press, Lahore, and published by R. P. Soni for Gandhi Publications League, Lahore.

* * * * *

Gandhi Series

BEHIND THE BARS

*

THIRD CLASS IN
INDIAN RAILWAYS
*

IN ROUND TABLE
CONFERENCE
*

Price Six Annas Each
AT ALL
RAILWAY AND OTHER BOOKSTALLS

www.ingramcontent.com/pod-product-compliance
Lightning Source LLC
Chambersburg PA
CBHW051340150726
47997CB00004B/1547